On Quiet Nights

poetry

Till Lindemann

Translated by Ehren Fordyce

RAW DOG SCREAMING PRESS

Published by Raw Dog Screaming Press
Bowie, MD

Cover & Interior Illustrations: © Matthias Matthies
Cover & Book Design: Jennifer Barnes
Author Photo: Bryan Adams

Printed in the United States of America

ISBN: 978-1-947879-94-2 / 978-1-947879-95-9

Library of Congress Control Number: 2015942436

www.RawDogScreaming.com

With illustrations from
Matthias Matthies

Contents

Translator's Note 7

Foreword 9

Symphony 18

Meaning 19

The Experiment 20

I love you 22

Father's Day 23

Elegy for Marie Antionette 24

When Mommy goes off late to work 26

Timeless 27

Important 28

Black 29

Love Song 31

Flesh 32

Dream 33

Not to live like a dog 34

Fear 36

So beautiful 37

Holidays 38

No 39

New Year's Eve 41

He and She 42

This I know 44

Why 45

No Heart 46

The Knife 47

We two 48

Stay 50

Hare Krishna 52

Origin of the Tides 53

I am not evil 54

Very often 55

Love makes blind 56

The whore.. 57
Alone 58
Logic 59
At Sea.. 60
Light... 62
Sunrise... 63
Spermtheft.. 64
I find I'm good.. 66
Unhoped for 67
Camping... 68
Nightingale 69
Slits.. 71
It's all wet.. 72
Eating leftovers... 74
Nothing 76
Who is it 77
Never 78
Only 79
Fresh snow 80
Miss June... 83
Red hair... 84
Roses.. 86
Sing for me.. 87
'Tis Pity.. 88
Beauty.. 89
Jump... 90
Animal friend.. 92
Decision... 94
Be quiet.. 95
In the country.. 96
Odd.. 98
Work week 99
The beautiful person... 100

Every night.. 101

Milk... 103

Where is your heart 104

Bigger Better Harder................................ 106

Spring.. 108

Alegria 109

Childhood.. 110

What I love... 111

Sweat... 112

Midnight 114

Very lonely with fish 116

True joy 118

The violin 120

Blood 122

Amsterdam 124

A ground 125

Do it.. 126

Warm day.. 127

A good idea.. 129

11:30.. 131

All.. 132

Naked.. 133

The bat 134

Eat this.. 135

Think broadly 137

Yes 138

A sight... 139

Neighbor's Son.. 140

Love... 141

Art... 143

Birthday... 144

Silhouettes.. 145

Translator's Note

In translating the poems from *On Quiet Nights*, I have sought as much as possible to keep the original rhyme structure and meter for those poems that are rhymed. In a few instances, for instance "Love Song," I abandoned the rhyme, partly due to the difficulty of conveying the style and grammar of the German (a series of infinitives ending in unstressed beats), but primarily because the literal meaning seemed to work well as a prose poem. As in any translation, compromises were made— sometimes emphasizing the meaning over the verse, sometimes approximating the meaning of the original to maintain the poetic structure. The German original occasionally plays with off-rhymes, as well as deviates from strict scansion, for reasons both of variety and emphasis. I have tried to emulate these qualities, although in attempting to preserve simultaneously meaning, rhyme and meter, it has probably been most difficult to carry over directly from German to English the sardonically conversational deviations in rhythm. As a result, the English may from time to time be a bit more sing-songy than the German. Additionally, the German often cuts the first syllable of a line, and in doing so, frequently drops the "I" preceding some verb phrase. This creates a (sometimes affectionately) brusque tone in the poems that I associate with barsch and schroff (crusty and gruff) Berliner German. Hopefully some of that humorously angular quality remains in the English.

Foreword

Till Lindemann: Growling in the Night
by Michael A. Arnzen

You hold in your hands a great poetry collection by a German rock icon, and I'm going to guess that you found this American edition and English translation because you're fully aware that the author—Till Lindemann—is the lead singer of uber-metal band, Rammstein. This translation of his poetry into English (by Ehren Fordyce, who did a masterful job of making English words rhyme the way the German ones did) is a unique publishing event, and something worth taking stock of.

In Germany, Rammstein's popularity is without question. This is a band that speaks to its generation, and the German people of Till Lindemann's generation—especially those born in the 60's and 70's—to be blunt, "get it." It's not fascist chant music; it's defiance and deviance, personified. I once read an interview where Lindemann said that, basically, his band was writing the equivalent of fairy tale stories for a world that has given up on fairy tales. And even in songs as wacky and insane as "Amerika" I can see the truth in that explanation. Rammstein punches through the bullshit, and gives us an avenue into archetypal longings and desires. And though Americans are not as fully aware of Rammstein as they should be, in much of the country the band is still respected by many a metalhead, despite the obscurity of its lyrics and messages, which are lost on so many who do not know the language, but appreciate the band's original and unforgettable sound.

Which is another way of saying: one of the most impressive achievements of Rammstein is that their music has caught on among Americans, despite the language barrier. The American music scene has always been somewhat isolationist—if not downright self-centered—in its affinity for English-only lyrics, despite its multicultural population. But once an American is lucky enough to discover Rammstein, they are floored. You have to respect a band which can get Americans banging their heads while chanting in unison with languages they cannot normally speak and probably do not really understand. *There is no stronger proof that there must be more to their words than simply their meanings*…and there is: Rammstein is a good band because they get the *sound* right. And Till Lindemann, the unmistakable voice of Rammstein and creator of so many of their lyrics, is mostly responsible for this success…because he is, at root, a great poet.

Poetry is about sound as much as it is about sense. Rammstein reaches a worldwide audience because Till Lindemann's lyrics cut across cultures; the sound they make is as universal as any scream or howl, and Till's vocalization of these words with all their Germanic trills and spittle express the feelings we all share—from rage to fear to lust—at the very level of their utterance. In some songs, Rammstein sneaks a little English into the mix, maybe to throw Americans a bone— as in "Amerika" or "Pussy"—songs that are hilarious in their mockery of nationalistic arrogance mixed with a brash sexuality that suggests one country might be screwing with another. But ultimately, vocabulary is less important to these American fans than the charge they feel in their ribcages when the music plays and Lindemann pushes his voice into the mic. One only needs to hear Till growl out the opening phrase that launches the song, "*Ich Will*"—a phrase delivered like a hot burp of molten tar mixed with broken glass—to know what I'm talking about: this is a voice to be reckoned with. And it's at the foundation of this collection of poetry.

In the metal scene, if Rob Halford is the best screamer of vengeance ever to pick up a microphone, then Till Lindemann is the best growler of unvarnished desire to ever spit fire. I think of him as a sort of Iggy Pop at his most intense, cranked up to the twentieth power. Till's throat sometimes bellows like a heavy fist, clenching and unclenching, the emotional undercurrent roiling like that of a man on the verge of going ballistic. It's metal because it's the voice of fury, deep and dark and dangerous. Yet unlike many Industrial acts, Till never lets go of the humanity that drives this demonic energy. At times he pines deeply heartfelt on the microphone (the song "*Ohne Dich*" ("Without You") will melt any icy heart with its *sturm und drang* sonic drama even as it conjures wastelands of frozen existentiality); at other times, he gleefully mocks himself and others with a dark sense of parody ("Amerika" is a riot). His voice humanizes the fuzz and fizzle of electronic distortion, harmonizes and enhances the pounding beats, giving them purpose—and it's hard to imagine the fury of these notes being delivered any other way.

That voice is here in this poetry, with its punchy delivery, its fascination with violence, sex, and the inevitable darkness of death. I think it helps to know your Rammstein to read this book. But there is much more going on here than the emotional current of aggressive metal. The words are carefully chosen and each well-crafted line invites you to sit with it for a while, musing over the irony, sadness or quirkiness of humanity. I dare say this is a collection of "love poetry"— Lindemann uses the word "heart" more than anyone I've read in a long time—but it never falls into drippy, stupid sentimentality. Every "heart" in this book reveals its wet scars and throbs with pain or bleats with blood in a genuine way. It's intelligent, but also *organic*.

Setting aside the raw lyrical power of the music that also throbs and bleats beneath these lines, and just reading Lindemann on his own terms, as a poet, this collection put me in the mind of the libertines. I'm reminded of the rakish burlesque of John Wilmot (Earl of Rochester), the ironic satire of Jonathan Swift and the libertarian values of the decadent movement from a century or more ago. The focus on grotesque bodily fluids throughout this book drives this point home (there's a tribute to "Sweat" in here, for instance; another celebrates the joy of pissing in the water). But I feel the libertine spirit really comes to the fore in the frankly sexual poems in this collection, whether in overt expressions of ejaculation—like "Spermtheft"—or in slightly more subtle depictions of the sex act—like "Dream." Hilariously tongue-in-cheek, at times sexually brutal, there's always also something confessional and intimate to these pieces, which muse over the calling of all flesh. This is not perversity so much as it is philosophy: Lindemann invokes the absurdities of the body through lewd word puzzles that raise intellectual quandaries about what separates man from animal, love from lust, man from woman. And when he's not reminding us of man's animal side, he's tearing down the artificiality of culture that gets in that animal's way (like in "Bigger Better Harder," a critique of plastic surgery for its own sake, written in a catalogue of grotesque body modifications that reminds me of Swift's "The Lady's Dressing Room").

Sometimes Lindemann waxes romantic in ways that may be hard to take seriously at first blush in comparison to the more bawdy works in this collection—as in "We Two"—until you see the gentle appreciation for simple love on display here, and give him the benefit of the doubt. And just as you begin to feel sympathy, the poem starts to unravel, and you soon realize there may be something *either* innocent *or* sinister about the love between man and animal depicted in the poem's final lines—and perhaps the point is that we are at once *both* pure and corrupt. This tension between our primitive animal selves and our rational human selves is essential to understanding what he is up to in this book, I think. The ambiguous meanings and ambivalent endings of poems like these make for compelling reading.

It's also, at the same time, raucous, rocking, fun. There's a lot of sputum and horror and meat in these poems—and Till "pokes fun" by poking you in the eye socket sometimes, rather than in the belly—but Lindemann's lusty provocations are far less scatological than they might seem on the surface. They seem to confess the intimacies of desire in a way that feels genuinely personal and sometimes deeply erotic, as in "Love Song," where the narrator wants to do all sorts of grotesquely intimate things with his lover's eyeballs. This is the nature, he suggests, of love: it is all-consuming at its best, and the terror and thrill of that desire is something we all have felt, even if Lindemann takes our imagination to places we seldom would explore openly in public. Ultimately, Till Lindemann takes risks that most contemporary writers wouldn't dare, and I really admire that. The exhibitionism on display here—similar to some of the dildo daring-do antics of Rammstein live on stage—make for provocative and rewarding musing.

At other times, Lindemann is cleverly playing with language, rhyme and meter to generate insight in ways that only the best poets really can. Nowhere is this clearer than in the very simple, and probably perfect, little poem, "The Knife"—in which the narrator takes a simple description of a breakfast scene and implies all sorts of "cover ups" going on, spread like butter by the dangerous instrument of the title. Some poems are so tight and short they read like abandoned song choruses from a potential Rammstein song (like the brilliantly structured single stanza of "Never": "There is no place/there is no space/and no room either"—three lines followed by an echoing triptyich of phrases crowded into its clever final line: "for you for me for ever." Brilliantly done.)

Lindemann is masterfully playful with song-like structure in many of these poems, revealing his innate musical talent in new ways that rock-and-roll simply won't allow. A good example of this might be the poem "Black," which references a commonly known children's bedtime prayer in Germany, "*Mude bin Ich, geht zur Ruh,*" (the English equivalent of "Now I Lay Me Down To Sleep"). He alludes to this nursery rhyme in form and content, ultimately twisting the sing-songy meter into a pensive depiction of the turning point from childhood to adulthood, in a sense, dramatizing the "dawn" of an all-consuming "dark" side. "Black" is not the only example of cultural referencing in Lindemann's work. Throughout this collection, there are any number of puns and whimsical allusions to "ye olden times" that play with our assumptions about what poetry can and should be—like in the rhyming poem, "Alone," where the narrator sounds like a puckish rake addressing a "fair maid" with a knowing wink before waxing about the emptiness of relations both "fruitful" (*fruchtbar*) and "frightful" (*furchtbar*). This penchant for word play, like the allusions to the past, seek meaning in language and stories of the past (those forgotten fairy tales I mentioned earlier), but ultimately he reveals how language and history fail to encapsulate the truth: to be "lonesome even as twosome" is still to be both "some" thing and "no" thing in that poem's final line (literally "*man allein*" (one alone). This loneliness pervades many of the poems, even those where Lindemann's narrator's seem content in their selfishness—like the parody of narcissism we find in the poem, "I Find I'm Good." The narrator falls in love "at first damn sight" with himself in the mirror. Perhaps, given Lindemann's background, this is not so much about selfhood as it is a critique of celebrity culture, told from an insider's view, through a mirrored lens.

In fact, many of these poems seem to turn inward and comment on music, performance and showmanship overtly. The collection opens with "Symphony," an inscrutable critique of "you violins, you trumpets" which blow empty like "the hole in my arse"—a poem that might not make much sense without our knowledge that the author is a celebrated musician. It would be a mistake to read this poem as a criticism of classical music—I see it as an indirect commentary on how the celebrity culture can "trump up" any asshole with their shit (black mass)—though at the same time it is "my" arse that "strolls in." Like "I Find I'm Good," the double-entendres in these poems always seem to critique the self as much as those they criticize.

Some of the poetry in this book is made up of a few simple lines that seem to rhyme for rhyme's sake, but they really do sound cool, just like a great musician might plunk out a few neat riffs while idly practicing backstage. [I would note here that some may have lost some of their meaning in English translation (as in "The Bat," which in its original version rhymes "*geschmeckt*"—to taste good—with "*gesteckt*"—to be stuck—and which may be making allusions to literature and cultural idioms that are beyond readers like me)]. But at other times, music becomes an unmistakable symbol of rage and vengeance. (What are we to make of the recurring chorus of "sing for me" when the song is the scream of an animal set ablaze? Or the ghostly woman's song that haunts the narrator of "Every Night"? Or even the "gruesome symphony" that concludes "The Violin"?)

Till Lindemann's collection will soon absorb you, and the time has come for me to shut up and let this book sing for itself. There are many poems in here that you might take a liking to. One poem I enjoyed a lot is "Very Lonely With Fish," in which a suicidal man plunges his head into an aquarium and muses pensively over the way the fish ignore the whole situation. At the penultimate moment of his demise, he notes, "the world is not the words you speak." That line sang to me. I think this phrase may summarize Lindemann's theme in this collection: that words have their limits, even as they enable you to imagine the world in unlimited and different ways, and perhaps the world is ultimately indifferent to our desires. But we must, defiantly, desire anyway.

The title of this collection probably derives from the opening line of the poem called, "Love": "On quiet nights there cries a man (*In stillen Nachten weint ein Mann*) / For remember still he can (*weil er sich erinnern kann*)." The man cries, because he can remember (something... Is it love? A better time? Or is he unable to forget what he did that caused this unbearable silence?). I like to think he also cries perhaps solely because he *can* cry out loud and that is enough to defy the darkness of quietude and to answer the indifference of nature. This defiance is Till Lindemann in a nutshell. He's not crying and not necessarily pining about "love," either. Rather, he's *growling*. And I know what he's saying.

Ich will….

You will enjoy singing along with him in these pages. Get to it, *ohne mich.*

Symphony

Black mass to my ear
You violins you trumpets
Let me live high and low
Did the hole in my arse
Stroll in

Meaning

You people look here
my life seems hard
I lie and steal
betray misdeal
yet tomorrow early I'll arise
treasures packed for southern skies

The Experiment

See it they will
They all stand still
See only see
It flamingly
At university
Failed
The experiment
Burns like parchment
The student stands still
In protest
Holds the fire fast
When the roof falls
There is only cement
And starry firmament
That is fine

You do not have to play with fire
If what you need is something warm
Burns lucent
The student

I love you

How could you even dream
that I would say to you
what I hardly dare think

Father's Day

Day by day and hour by hour
your blood runs through my veins
in minutes and seconds
thinned with fear and cold tears
in your solitude you fare
alone on the high seas
and call words to me in the wind
that I do not understand

Where are you

Have your eyes with which to see
I know you
do not know you
carry your blood here and there
I know you
know you no more
in your solitude you fare
alone on the high seas
and stand before me nights in dream
the hurt you did recedes

Where are you

Elegy for Marie Antionette

Madame
Shall be disposed to know
A quite horrid fate faces she
Soon before the common ranks
From her head she will be free
That's history
at any rate
Hereafter may I thee penetrate
In the wordhole over thine chin
I remember thee well therein

The steel falls and without grace
The head rolls lays out in space
Without body and without hat
Still warm plenty good for that
Fleshstem stands surveys the city
Ah it would be such a pity
But decency strikes virtue's code cuts

Better sing-songily
Than not to be

When Mommy goes off late to work

When Mommy goes off late to work
I stay at home alone
She tosses me a biscuit
Then locks me in my room

When Mommy goes off late to work
She does not go by train or bus
Her working quarters aren't so far
It is the room just next to us

Here they come and there they go
Sometimes two at once arrive
The late birds love to sing and crow
And what if Mommy cries

When she sends me early off to bed
She says I shouldn't cast a gloom
Then weeps until her face burns red
And locks me in my room

Here they come and there they go
The light in the window red
I'm looking through the keyhole
And one has knocked her dead

I was already sad before
Mommy's not gone to another place
I sniff upon her knickers
And put makeup on my face

Timeless

I'm a dandy cobbler's boy
Out to resole the world
Alas my love of life has stolen
All my time left over

Important

Three times daily eat and sup
Post and pee now don't mess up
At Christmastime donate a buck
And once a week be sure to fuck

Black

In search of peace before night's fall
I drape myself in melancholy's shawl
The bright world doesn't beatify me
Got to have darkness for my ecstasy

It's the pregnant-with-the-dead night
Enrapts us to a sinner's plight
Commandments that we disrespect
Are seen by none in dark's neglect

After the last rays
The soul gets lost in lust strays
Then I enjoy the sun's demise
Drink the black with deepening sighs

Daylight's loss leaves all the rest
For whom the night holds out her breast
Drinkers, whores and conspirators
For them the shadows' open doors

When day holes up inside the moon
A fever stirs the bones we swoon
No pretend candle here in the heart
No prayer to set light and dark apart

After the last rays
The soul gets lost in lust strays
Then I enjoy the sun's demise
Slurp the black with deepening sighs

Love Song

Your eyes
I would gladly take them in my mouth
Constantly to suck on them to lick
By all means to hang them from my balls
To stick them under my foreskin
To lay them wet on my breast
To sing them love songs
Both in the anus would be a blessing
To squeeze them in the armpits
To sew them on my tired eyes
Till life leaves me
For the eyes to see into the eyes
And hold them fast upon my lips

Flesh

I found flesh in the garden
Turned out to be a stone
Not something one could eat
But fine for a window when thrown

I found flesh in the yard
It wallowed in the dreck
Wanted to knock it hard
It ran away like heck

I found flesh in the bed
It had a face on it
Thought it must be love
Wasn't worth a sonnet

Dream

Me a lad her already old
But skin still soft and mellow
In her shadow it was warm
Her flesh a waxy yellow

Me a lad her already old
For both love's need for the other
Sick from youth I asked for her
Didn't leave me long to suffer

She held me firmly by the teeth
The tongue was hoisted high
Her mouth went up and then went down
But kissed me not one time

And fine upon my skin
A rain came down to lay
On shuddering depths of youth
Where my heart was turning gray

Warm upon my dream
A rain came down to lay
Was woken from fine shudder
All flecked with baby spray

Not to live like a dog

Someone tore the legs off the dog
because he pissed on the piano
in his need the cur makes a gift of his chain
gives it to God
who rewards so much generosity
lets the dog legs grow again
then the brute jumps on the piano and craps on the keys
the Lord God is disappointed
but cannot punish
his chain holds him to the good

Fear

The sunflower is parched
stands there dying at the window
cries its last yellow in the room
it is a sad thing to follow

I turn away full of fear

Old and dried and long forgotten
all the splendor gone so quickly
to me as well this pain will happen
yesterday was yet so lovely

So beautiful

Lay your face
on a sheet of paper
it's already a poem
and will live

Holidays

Tears are not to be seen in water
nor tasted if you drown in the drink
they are mixed in with other tears
while to the ocean's ground you sink

No

My worthy heart
it sings no more
not that there's something to be sad for
some sharp syllable cut nicely
in the bosom still and empty
now it is fractured and lovesore
and does not beat so dutifully
not that there's something to be sad for
my heart just weighs a wee bit more
and not that there is any sorrow
from my ducts the tears drippingly
respond only to the smoke

give me another cigarette

New Year's Eve

Sometimes it doth occur to me
as I am far younger than thee
That I should cast you so it holds
And pour some lead into your folds

He and She

He: Why are you hitting me
She: Don't know
He: Fine
He: Why are you hitting me
She: Am bored
He: All right then
He: Why are you hitting me
She: Am lonely
He goes and buys a dog
Dog: Why are you hitting me

She: Who built this wonderful house for us
He: An architect breeds dogs
Dog bays
He: Keep an eye out
Dog: What for? Isn't anything

She: I am having a child
He: You have to press
She presses
He: That hurts
Dog laughs

He: But it's ugly
She: It says nothing
She hits the child
Child: I say nothing
Dog bites the child
Child: So I'm alive then

She: Help me put it on
He: Have you washed
Dog: Let me on the tits once too

She: Who built that beautiful house
House shakes itself and throws all the tiles from its roof
He: I am dying
She: I am dying too
Dog takes Child on its back
Child: Keep going straight ahead

This I know

I know the sun
The sun knows me not
Will burn my face
As soon as it is hot
This I know

I know the little hare
The little hare knows me not
The dog gets the head
The rest in the pot
This I know

I know the father
And father knows me back
He bangs the mother
On back and stomach slaps
This I know

Why

When evenings are by moonlight
the tiny fish begin to teem
it draws me down to water
to see our ringlet in the stream

Deep from my breast I tore it out
A circle made of blood and silver
You were the diamond set on top
And a child held out its finger

She gave me just a final kiss
Then threw the ring into the brook
The child I will forever miss
I stand on the bridge and look

When nights around our little ring
The tiny fish begin to press
Then I lay the rounded moon
On the hole within my chest

No Heart

Cold fingers in the neck
I found you by red light
You without a heart
Me love at first sight

I took you back to my place
Sewed up your wound
I searched for your heart
Was nowhere to be found

Beneath your breast I smelled
And sought many an hour
Complete inside you crawled
But no heart to discover

Born without a heart were you
Or did you lose it in the dew
Were you once torn by love apart
Maybe stabbed within the heart
Or did it simply go to ground
It's something I have never found
You have no heart

The Knife

The knife put spread on a heart
Everyone was there and their mother
I watched too
As pains got covered
In scrambled eggs and butter

We two

We two
Equibalanced equipoised
You crawled into my heart
We two

I am I
And you are you
Mutely fate does watch us two
I am good this way
This way good to you
And when I speak
You listen too
Come near
Come to me here
We two
Equibalanced equipoised
You flew into my heart
We two
You never yet untrue

I give you straw
I give you hay
I love you
True to you I stay
On the field in the pen

Everywhere they seek us then
But never will they find us
Our wingèd backs do bind us
One day we shall ascend on high
To find our sheep's cloud in the sky

Stay

Lies still in my arm
I cannot have enow
nursery for lice and sperm
my good old pillow

Hare Krishna

I make my pain a gift to you
I subdue myself through and through
For you my bare foot I do dip
Into a river full of shit
Great spirit now make me believe
Heaven's reprieve is there for me
Since I have a lot of karma
Lead me home to my nirvana

Into the river I bleed in haste
Twixt body parts and body waste
A ribbon red adorns my torment
Appears to me in lustrous garment
Great spirit now make me believe
Heaven's reprieve is there for me
For I have a lot of karma
Hare Krishna Hare Rama

See but how the pain is bright
At once I am now full of light
See how the pain begins to be
When it shows itself to me

Origin of the Tides

There once was a fisherman
who threw his heart into the lake
the water did not give it back
his breast in two did break
in wrath he tore the stars from night
the water short withdrew from sight
then waves drove blind across the land
the helpless streams did break their bands
the high tides wept most furiously
the salty seas did come to be
from fisher's hand one star was torn
a sentry fire left on shore
among the strayed hearts

I am not evil

I am not evil
I am just not really good
I am not bad
I am just not a good person

What is not good
Is not right or very good or bad
What is not bad
That is good or very bad or dead

How I love my life
Loves me like a falling knife
Kicks me in the cojones
Slaps me 'cross the face

How I hate adversity
But adversity loves me
Seeking an embrace
Always giving chase
I run away try to get loose
But it pulls me back
Draws me close

I am not evil
I am just not exactly good
I am not bad
I am just not a good person

Very often

One times one legs uncross
Two times mad senses lost
Three times child dropped in moss
Thousand times my heart to dust

Love makes blind

Love is a light
That makes your face shine bright
Out your pores it doth unwind
So over time I'm slowly blind
And it comes as a surprise
When you I no more recognize

The whore

Dear soul
curse to bear
given neither scarf nor hair
love set on you its frozen band
coiled round with unseen hand
now to choose which less is best
cold delight or hot distress
I want to love but also live
not in murky doubt misgive
the frozen band I've torn away
and shat upon that white-furred beast
made old by reason day by day
I now forever after acquiesce
to be the whore of my loneliness

Alone

Fair maid
Would you be averse
To my carrying your purse
Your innocence seems a little tainted
So be my first and get acquainted
All seems so fruitful at the start
But will be frightful ere they part
The woman evades
The man invades
Lonesome even as twosome

Logic

What goes in
Also comes out again
What comes out
Also goes in again
What does not go in
Is too big

I come back out again

At Sea

Seaman, leave the women
Women still at home
Seaman sails singly
Off abroad alone
Love is an ocean and I
want to ply every sea
Why should I hold to one
When I can have many

Light

Turn the light on
So that I thee
May look upon

Sunrise

Once the day has killed the moon
It blushes red before the dew
Somehow ashamed not quite at ease
The birds are giggling in the trees

Spermtheft

The agèd flesh in carnival
Indulges hips without chagrin
The kissing sickness spreads o'er all
And skin just wants to hug on skin
Give my bodylust some scope
Pores are weeping under hairs
The animal breaks off its rope
Will goes ill
Sprays its wad
Yes the seed breaks from the pod
Then the fragrance starts

Look down
No more is it within
I do believe I've come again

I find I'm good

I did not think it possible
I love my self something awful
I could not stand upon my feet
when I my mirrored me did meet
quickly sat down on a seat
soon I and I were friends complete
I knew my destiny all right
love it was at first damn sight

A handsome devil I am not
but character I've got a lot
fair image in a lousy frame
my splendid seed is all my fame
and see how fine my hair doth lie
I do not walk in truth I fly
So I roam from cloud to cloud
A sky apart the madding crowd

I find I'm good I taste quite good
in flacons belongs my lovely blood
I'm also rich and very wise
respected for my bedroom eyes
while now and then a heart doth break
with women I communicate
if everyone were more like me
the world would be in harmony

Unhoped for

I simply could not refuse her anything
till that day
now I have to go to prison

Camping

A nail that falls into the eye
such pain to me another's bliss
two sweating bodies unify
one tries to stay aloof from this
then slowly one begins to cry

Nightingale

Once I heard a nightingale
By day I hear her plaint
I throw an estimable stone
The feathered beast is slain

I take myself to the dead beast
And then I start to weep
I lay its heart onto my breast
Its head in mine to sleep

While west the corpse lies in my maw
her voice is twinned within the craw
And to my grief two voices screech
I grab new stones now one for each

Behind its bars bedecked with skin
I hold my captive heart locked in
My soul a hardened pistol grip
From out the barrel's womb it slips
Desire cries from every pore
Damnation
downfall evermore

Slits

Slits slits slice slice
for me it's better with a knife
for me a knife is always good
out the flesh doth leap the blood
the skin is nicely opened wide
a purple color dots the bride
like a beast who's wet her whine
I wish another now were mine
crying softly crying loud
warm friend to whom my trust I've vowed
I feel as though I've just been born
in tiny ships upon your pores
my ancient sorrow, heavy freight
is softly sailing through the night
it's pitched and tossed on reddish tide
the newest scar still waits outside
many hours in wait it laid
so in joy the body flayed

It's all wet

When the fat man takes a bath
opened legs and beer on tap
the cellar when the pipes have broke
bedsheets after a good long poke
Red Sea Dead Sea fish in a net
When I cry 'cuz I'm upset

It's all wet

Ships that founder and then sink
Those who drown within the drink
All genres of libation
Bloodletting and lactation
When my passport I forget
Washed in pants to my regret

It's all wet

When I piss and lose my bearing
Or gas within requires airing
A comely lass that my tongue laps
A blanket wanked and nicely waxed
When I kiss a streetwise strumpet
Or poorly blow upon a trumpet

It's all wet

Yes the anus and the crack

If I sit and flush, my back
Rain upon a pane of glass
The throat I tell the dog: catch!
In the sauna when I sweat
And the panties of Barbette

It's all wet

Eating leftovers

Your leftovers I may ingest
Something you forgot – here it is
I want to bow and have my joy
Yes make my body into your toy
You torture beasts and me too
A fire set inside my sinew
My little body spoiled with blows
Beat it with love red as a rose
Your discontent shows on your face
No hitting girls it seems to say
Then is many an hour *triste*
When you refuse to play the beast
Desire stands now unrequited
You resent the feelings I've incited
I love something that you dislike
Who knows how long our love will bide

To be nought for you
Is blessing
And when I then have died,
for you I'll still be living

Nothing

Nothing will ever happen to you
I say in the moment
So perfect
and extol all time
there where blood squeezes into my hose
from which you too soon can live

Whether in light or shadow
only lay the ear on the fleshstream
harken to its purity
it murmurs its delta
will wind its finger in you

Who is it

Just who is it who speaks with me
it is not you unfortunately
the word rolls sweet it's something else
oh God I'm speaking with myself

Never

There is no place
There is no space
And no room either
For you for me for ever

Only

What does one lose
in the blink of an eye?
The moment?
Many, time
Some, consciousness
Several, life

Fresh snow

Like an animal I slunk to her
Bowed by lust somehow altered
Felt a stab pierce deep my heart
Me compared to her what a thought

She like fresh snow and I so old
I am formless she the mold
The message clear upon her face
You cannot have me don't give chase

Youthful hearts still smolder
While I have begun to molder
But should innocence step off her throne
I'll get a piece to call my own

I said to her, there is no pain
Some blood on snow but why refrain
The skin-upholstered nail was stuck
(deep in of course) the bud was plucked

A quiet scream a soft recoil
Canvas sunset done in oil
Blooming glory to frozen rose
And it snows it snows and snows

While youthful hearts still smolder
I'll get warm on what's left over
Should innocence step off her throne
I'll take a piece to call my own

Miss June

Nights in dream
you stand before me say
take my hand
and lead me far away

Red hair

Little girl do not worry
I give you a can of birds
in flames like the roof of your legs
nest under the arm
they sing the crap out of their crops
nestle in the fiery stink of the armpit
with a pig

Little girl do not worry
pig gobbles birds
now it can sing
we gobble the swine
is even fish inside
animals one may eat

Little girl can now sing
chokes on a fishbone dies
drowned in red hair

Roses

Behind all the blooming glory
Hidden
A nasty spine laughs sorry

Sing for me

I've brought some animals for you
From that hole
At the meadow's wet edge
Do you know
Where we found the little ring

Sing for me come sing
Hands without fingers
Sing for me o sing
The finger lacks the ring

Now ghastly fire in the night
The stovehole they ascend
The beasts we did ignite alight
And scream
still burning to the end

Sing for me come sing
A kitten holds the ring
Dance for me come dance
Puppydogs' tails do prance

'Tis Pity

She carries the heart on her tongue
Bit on it
Then the heart was split

Beauty

When roses in the garden bloom
the rosy sight evokes a spell
the sighing violets' soft perfume
conflated with the roses' smell

Jump

Into the dry grass we crawled
insect stung her began to bawl
began to spring with quivering thighs
among the brilliant butterflies
without dress and without bodice
breasts aloft like foreign bodies

Quietly I asked her then
whether she please
could do that once again
among the brilliant butterflies
began to spring with quivering thighs

Animal friend

I am an animal friend
Without doubt
Yet I want to play the angles
If with humans I don't succeed
I experiment with animals

Never can they cry
Never ever laugh
I stick to the little guys
And cut away the chaff
They pose no opposition
Never ask one question
Wish to be no burden
In all say nothing certain

I am an animal friend
That is clear
I love them wholeheartedly
Whether I flay them or I eat them
Be they savory or elderly
And it hurries on the cold night
Quick now quick bring the lamb
Inside and out of sight

I am an animal friend
Unto the end
Little hands with teeth to rend
Then gladly off to bed sedate
Decked in skins as it grows late
They've quite a lot of hairs
On their face and in the tail
To every little beast its treat
At laughing animals do fail

Decision

A gunshot
made
by choice
now the brain spread
like a flower
on the forehead

Be quiet

Appetite spins round the mouth
Over the lips plays a twitch
Spittle swims towards the ear
Everything starts to itch
If only the tongue would scratch
Long I smelled the thing let it smart
Finally went and broke off a part
Then shoved each piece into its case
Tears one by one back in the face
Cloudy weather drawn through the flesh
Voilà a rainbow nice and fresh

In the country

She was cold-blooded but well-bred
Time for us was without stress
By the lilacs white I touched her head
Confused by loneliness

We agreed immediately
And ran down to the willow
The skin was soft and wrinkly
Where limbs split into furrow

It is so still
When a heart goes crack
Thinking that this must be love
And not just lack
Dusted with shame
With lust aflame
It is quite still
When a heart gets smacked

Now snug upon the saddle horn
And what's this taste of turf
Too soon the night becomes the morn
Quick hide the hairs within the earth

I barely held her by the rein
She was promised only me
Desire sought to break its chain
And mounted briskly up my knee

It is so still
When a heart goes crack
Even if I do not want to
One must simply love her
I thought this is love
And not just lack
It is quite still
When a heart gets smacked

Odd

How odd the slipping into day
You to be or not – what do we say
How odd the slipping into night
I brought you under me all right

Today is washed in evening's dusk
Tomorrow I leave you with the dust
The hoi polloi should not forget
Which one of us our Maker's met

Work week

There are tools
for the cutting apart
of body parts
which I like
I clean them
and sharpen them
every Thursday
it makes for me
and my comrade fingers
a weekend

The beautiful person

The beautiful person
Is beautiful no more
Hair gone, flesh burned
Ugly now to look upon
We wonder what went on
Somehow it all went west
Black powder white vest

Every night

And whether I was slung in sleep
That night her song she sung for me
Rustled in from way off far
A susurration from a star
And whether I was weft in sleep
Some tingling drew me to my feet
To the willow down it leads my ears
I've had enough it disappears
She was for me long forgotten
And yet I once was so besotten
I call her name into the room
And sleep no more can only fume
My breast encaged within a fence
Apparently I must repent

Milk

The dark is there the dark is not
Devoid of light the bud breaks out
She came at night with pale white skin
With my mouth I took her in

Where is your heart

Down to the horse I led her mute
A touch of my hand upon her boot
She mounts the steed her legs apart
Into my lap descends my heart

Were you conceived without a heart
Or did you two decide to part
Up on the steed she seems suspended
Up on the steed the earth's upended
Where is your heart

A little dream of bliss concluded
A glance from her no I'm deluded
She vainly sits there on that nag
She says my name like it's a drag

And once astride the humble beast
She does not ride she flies released
One form one life a single source
The rideress upon her horse

Did someone come and break your heart
A stranger stab and leave you scarred
Up on the steed she seems suspended
Up on the steed the earth's upended
Where is your heart

Along her trail I meekly crept
Until her horse did break its neck
Down in a copse deep in the wood
And neither horse nor pride withstood

In a break of wind on the earth's skin
I build us a bed to lie within
And long I lick upon her face
Her bloodless lips will give no place

I'm mounting up begin to sing
I make her gallop round the ring
The reins held fast the saddle hard
I gaze upon her disregard

Where is your heart
Did it disappear before its time
I look and look and nothing find
Up on the steed she seems suspended
Up on the steed the earth's upended
Where is your heart

Bigger Better Harder

Seven kilos slim aesthetic
Knife and swab and anaesthetic
Cut the eyes back sack reduction
Rhinoplasty liposuction
Pull the ears a little tighter
Double chin a wee bit lighter
With thread and needle scissors light
One takes the pain without a fight

Although your tits are not too small
They should be larger all in all
Tooth extraction *dans la face*
Implantations in the ass
Tighten cheeks cheekbone displace
Lips made plump with special waste
With thread and needle scissors light
One takes the pain without a fight

Wrinkles scalpeled not a trouble
Penis lengthened up to double
Him so happy with his stiffy
Sex adjusted in a jiffy
The woman in the man confused
The hairs that one will never lose
With thread and needle scissors light
One takes the pain without a fight

Spring

The sun no longer hides in shame
the winter wishes to recline
turns home again to his muddy bed
falls asleep with noisy yawn
March commences to strum a chord
the horizon line is one long string
a nightingale provides support
begins flamboyantly to sing

Alegria

One feels as though one's at a fair
The thickened blood the muggy air
The girls are young the wine is old
The days are hot
The nights aren't cold
The veins are humming with some drug
The teeth have hairs from chewing rug
The heart from out its cage will spring
And can you hear the tenors sing
The good old things recall *España*
Latin- and sud-americania

Childhood

The sap still drips the tree still lives
although the bark is deeply scratched
the scabs and scurf persist as signs
the soul to early wounds attached

What I love

I do not love that I love something
Do not like it when I like something
I am not pleased
when I am pleased
Yet I know
I will regret it

A happy me is not to be
The one who loves me must agree

What I love must go on dying
Will decay there's no denying
From joy and bliss will come affliction
Redemption calls for crucifixion
What I love
must go on dying

Sweat

It is the way that I was born
With pools of pores beneath my arm
Wee beasts go drowning in the drink
For every day I'm bound to stink

Perspiring comes unprovoked
My hair and clothing always soaked
Till weirs and islands start to form
This news just in my skin is storm

The sun casts off its goodly rays
My body mists and starts to haze
Tenaciously cascading down
My sweat descends to flood the ground

And if I think to times ahead
Of me upright or flat in bed
My sweat remains a thing foretold
No matter that I'm freezing cold

It's unbelievable I know
Out my eyes the sweat doth flow
I make excuses, say it's tears
In shame retreat, avoid my peers

I dress in black but not from woe
The women come but always go
A wet outsider till the end
My sweat will even death transcend

Midnight

So how describe the image right
there's him the window pane the night
he's pressed his face against the glass
and hopes that soon she'll light a match

Never seen her, nakedly
the mistress of his fantasy
he takes the glasses from his eye
and trembling sings himself a line

Midnight's here at last it's come
from you I steal away the sun
for always in the dark it is
that moon and sun begin to kiss

The breath cuts short the heart beats fierce
the picture by the paintbrush pierced
the pane is fogged but then it's still
a dribble on the windowsill

The view for him is well-disposed
horizon to the vault disclosed
he saddles up his fantasy
and conjures her anatomy

His eyes unleash that lavish spark
the blaze rekindled in the dark
with sweating thoughts and speed lightwhite
they travel on into the night

The dark has taught its lesson well
How joy is caught by setting fire
He journeyed up to heaven's gate
And hung new suns to his desire

Midnight's here at last it's come
from you I steal away the sun
for always in the dark it is
that moon and sun begin to kiss

Very lonely with fish

When the dusk descends
The sky slowly turns to stone
Then my heart contracts
And I feel I am alone

On a table in a room
Is standing an aquarium
Round a rock the fishies swim
And nibble on the scum

Down I dunk my head within
The fish aquarium
They could care less, so on they swim
Circling till they're numb

I hold my breath in for the sprint
My lungs are getting tight
I suck my cheeks in one more time
The fish could give a shite

And so it was I almost drowned
It's true I saw the light
Angels waved at me spellbound
The fish cared not a mite

The light is circumscribed by dark
The world is not the words you speak
Need a moral? A last remark:
Beware of whose respect you seek

True joy

Rejoice, you fool, I spread misrule
and piss into the swimming pool
for me it's like some Easter fête
to watch as one by one a guest
imbibes my urine by the liter
quaffs the juice of my St. Peter
like dandelions in the rain
they stare with eyes a gold champagne

The violin

My heart belonged to a violin
I stroked just her neck
when I was tired of leading
the bow in the morning
it sang alone for itself
the most beloved of all ballads
and I cried with the dogs
and ate the grapes only
from her brown skin

A piano cast a fatal spell on me
of black and white I so drunk
and ah so wide
opened was his beautiful mouth
sang so sadly like the autumn
I threw away the bow and then
the keyboard beast promised me fever

From then on the violin was out of tune
me to forgive she found no note
so she went soon from hand to hand
not one able to play her
and was broken and misused
on a winter day burned

Practiced my conducting
to drown my woe
in the deepest part of the orchestra pit
I am there crumpled on the stand
and go now
myself to ground
in gruesome symphony

Blood

Blood is good
When it
In your body swims
Blood is not good
When on your skin it thins

Rill dainty rill
In my veins spill

Between thistles
Under thorns
The blood froths beyond its bourns
On head and heel a crimson welt
I'm sorry because
I cannot give you any help

Who are you

Who are you
Show me who you are
Let us trade
I give you food
And you give me love
A little

With your feet you step on me
Out of my hand you feed
I pay your debts
Love is enflamed
Who are you

Amsterdam

There she sits stiff pink stays pulled back
Gaze arrested do not disturb
The street reeks of sweat and lilac
You can hear the growing herb
I stand stockstill below her sill
Shows her skin shame be damned
Her heart is there I see her will

Good morning Amsterdam

She washes me I lose my pride
A look escapes the captive eyes
She slowly starts to get inside
And flays me good I'm mesmerized
Rust my heart and rust my veins
Her hairy sponge scrubs hard yes ma'am
My sweet and salty tears she drains

Good morning Amsterdam

A ground

She says
tell me the reason
give me the grounds, it hurts me
I hang a park bench around her throat
she runs aground there
the park is beautiful and deep the sea

Do it

Caress my arm
caress my stomach
caress without objection
then too me down there
over the left limb
and the right limb
with sunshine I brim
so let the sun into your grave
I give to you a summer day

Warm day

The sun illumines women's skin
Seeps in sight without a din
Blinding like the freshest snow
It hurts my eyes my heart feels woe

When springtime tumbles out of March
Suns abound from women's hearts
The brain is bit the veins take wing
Oh my Lord the Sirens sing

A thousand pinpricks of desire
The hands are longing to acquire
Everywhere the ample flesh
Knees grows weak the skin grows flush

Completely helpless I have to watch
As baby sleeps in mama's crotch
Earth swells up and starts to swing
Oh my Lord the Sirens sing

In your loins it's creeping in
Smell of sex adrenaline
Tie me up and slug me down
Bind my eyes before I drown

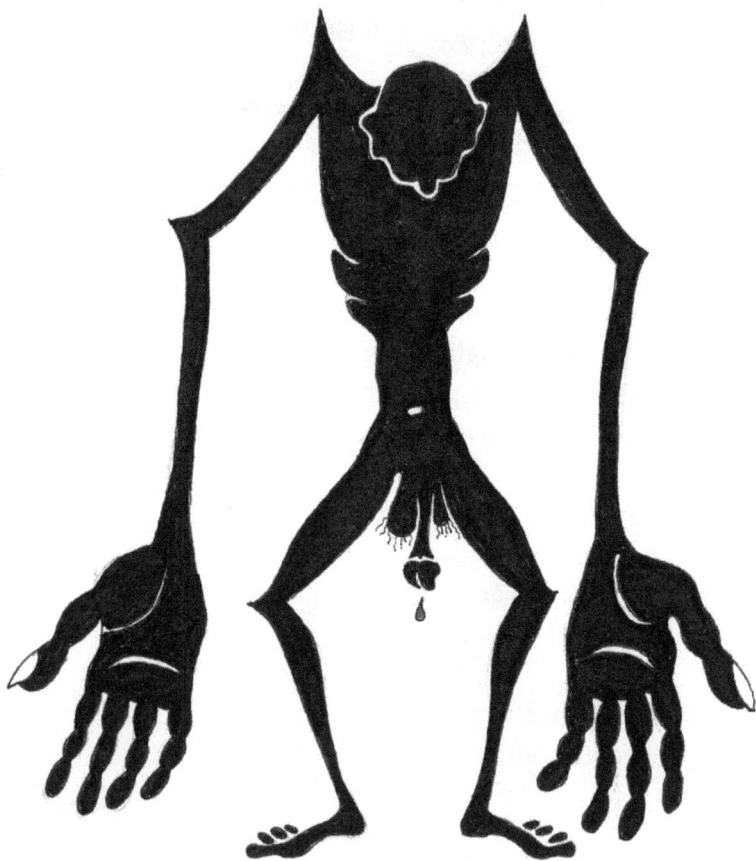

A good idea

Soon I will be dead
The end is long foretold
Soon you will forget me
By someone else consoled

There's no changing it
It's a stupid joke
But the thought alone
Makes we want to choke

Soon I will be dead
It stands fixed in the stars
When I am expired
You will briefly grieve
And after I am dead
To someone else you'll cleave

There's no changing it
It's a stupid joke
But I see one way out
You could also croak

11:30

I feel therefore
alas I am

All

A hose is there
the end open
and they waft into the all
no air
breathe one can beforehand

Naked

Nights in dream I take my lyre
And lead in song a vestal choir
Ten maidens at assembly
One century and seventy
Their naked love is all for me
Too bad this dream will never be

The bat

The bat from the pigeon coop
tasted good
basted with burnt wine
skewered on wood

Eat this

You should not cry
Eat my dreck drink my dreck
I am dirty will not go away
Eat my dreck drink my dreck
Suck it down lick it away
You should cry
The earth will hatch
Between my thighs
Tears in the grass

Think broadly

You say, I am too old for you
Now
We will see
True the tooth of time does gnaw on me
Yet
Dear child be sensible if you please
look at your mother
think broadly
what a good time means for me
mid-twenties that's clover
and the years that canopy over
you do not make the difference at the end
no question who laughs last or more
just look at your breasts those flat spent
stars that are falling to the floor
I've seen a thousand times before

Yes

A speedy word that yes
my faith to her I swore
we traveled to the sea
in sand our troth foresworn

A sight

Insight
a glance
into tomorrow
was not nice

Neighbor's Son

So who of you is up to ride me?
don't everybody disagree
a little wait and then the knock
the neighbor's son has come to talk
go on you skank now lick my yolk
then fix that fence you fucking broke

Love

On quiet nights there cries a man
For remember still he can

Art

It does really really good
when someone understands your art

Birthday

On your name day
I give you the gift of wings
Now climb on top the house
And jump
I'll blow the candles out

Silhouettes

Shadows are step-children to the sun
visited from time to time by the moon

Photo: Bryan Adams

About the Author

Till Lindemann was born in 1963 in Leipzig, the son of children's book author and writer Werner Lindemann and journalist Brigitte Lindemann. In his youth he was a competitive swimmer and was in line to go to the 1980 Olympics in Moscow but an injury ended his participation in the sport. He worked as an apprentice carpenter, a gallery technician, a peat cutter and a basket weaver. In 1994 he became singer and lyricist for Rammstein. He lives in Berlin. His first book of poems, *Messer*, was published in 2005. *On Quiet Nights* was originally published as *In stillen Nächten* in Germany in 2013.